MW00803848

THE PEACE
OF
THE
SOLOMON
VALLEY

MARGARET HILL McCARTER
Author of
"The Price of the Prairie,"
"In Old Quivira,"
"Cuddy's Baby,"Etc.

CHICAGO
A.C.McCLURG & CO.
1913

The Publishers' Press
Chicago

"The Peace of the Solomon Valley mingled with
the peace of our own hearts."

To the Good People
Of a Good Land
Even the Folks Who Dwell
In this Valley
With Deep Appreciation
Of Their Kind Words and Deeds
To Me-ward

"*If you're world-weary, and longing
    for rest,
Just come to the Plains and submit to
    be blessed.*"

LILLA DAY MONROE

THE PEACE OF THE SOLOMON VALLEY

MARCH

Letter from JOHN ELLERTON, New York City, to DANIEL BRONSON, Talton, Kansas.

NEW YORK CITY, *March.*

DEAR DAN:

The newspaper you sent last week was almost like a letter from you, because it was just like you to send the paper instead of writing the message it contained. You know how I welcome every bit of information concerning you and yours, but, of course, you'd never tell me how prosperous you are now. Left it for the *Talton Herald* to set forth how "Daniel Bronson, one of the well-to-do farmers up on the Solomon, shipped out"—how many carloads of cattle was it? And what is alfalfa coined out of anyhow, that it can bring in such a wad of money to a "well-to-do" farmer? Well-to-do! I should say so, with checks like the one the printer set up coming in with the shipment of stock and sale of that long-legged clover you call alfalfa. Did my heart good to read about it, though, just because your name went with it. I'll confess here that I was afraid at first to look through that newspaper for the blue pencil marks, for fear—oh, well, never mind.

7

We are not young any more. I suppose we must expect now that sometime one will be taken and the other left. I can't realize that we are both getting close to sixty, with children grown up. At least my boy thinks he is a man. And yet, Dan, it seems such a short time since we went out of Yale together, neck and neck for honors. You remember our planning to go West together? What care-free days those were! That was a glorious jaunt we took across the Plains back in the '70's. You stayed in Kansas because you wanted to and I came back to New York because I had to. But say, old man, you needn't fill your letters as you did your last one with what you say I did for you in your day of trouble out there. I only loaned you a few thousand dollars to tide you over the day of wrath when the drouth and grasshopper and mortgage fell on you as well as on the unjust. And you have paid me back every cent. You seem to forget that. I wonder where I would have been in that near-panic of 1907 if I hadn't had some good Kansas coin (coin you had minted out of your cattle and alfalfa) to invest when all the springs were running dry for us smaller fellows in the East.

But I'm writing now, Dan, to ask a favor of you. You remember how that rheumatism had me hobbled down when I went to Kansas thirty years or more

ago? You ought to, because you had to
carry me half the time. And you remember what six months in the Solomon Valley did for me? I came home
sound as a dollar and never had a twinge
of rheumatism since that summer. Now
my boy, Leroy, who finished Yale a
year ago, has been ailing with the same
accursed affliction for nearly two years.
It knocked him out of his athletics the
last year of his college course. It nearly
broke his heart, or what is worse, his
spirit. He wants me to send him off to
Europe. Dan, I can't afford it right
now, and I don't want to anyhow.
He's got the wrong notion about himself and the world. Rheumatism will
do that for a fellow. He thinks he is
going to be a confirmed invalid, a gentleman invalid, not able to earn, but
fully able to spend. And that's not all.
He does n't look at things plumb. New
York is all right as a place to make
money, but, like all big cities, it is a
poor place to make character in children. Why, this city'd go to smash if
all the New England, Indiana, and
Kansas country-bred boys were sud-
denly pulled out of its business circles.
But Roy's got the idea — you know his
kind, Dan,— that the Lord made the
world as far west as the Adirondacks,
maybe, and left the rest to chance. He's
fixed in the foolery that this city is the
centre of God's eternal universe.

I want to send him to you for six
months, first, to lose that rheumatism
and confirmed-invalid notion somewhere out there on the prairies, and second, to learn what the West and country life are worth. Can you stand him
for that time? You can let him learn
his lesson alone. He'll come to you
with some high and mighty notions
about the East and himself. If he
does n't come home next Fall a new man
it will be the disappointment of my life.

If our children could always lean on
us it would be easy sailing down the
years, but I'm up against the fact that
we must shape them up to live their own
lives, and that those lives may be in
marble halls or wayside hovels, with
Fate playing the strongest hand of cir-
cumstance against us.

Don't misunderstand Roy. He is a
gentleman clear to the bone. He con-
fides in me as much almost as in his
mother, who, by the way, agrees with
me only partially in this plan. I'm
proud of him, of course, but he must
learn that he's only a temporary invalid
and he must get a bigger perspective
on the country over which Old Glory
swings and on the folks that live under
the shadow of it. You know, Bronson,
how much I'll appreciate what you can
do for me.

I'm so concerned about Roy, I almost forgot to say that Mrs. Ellerton

has been called up to East Machias, Maine, to stay indefinitely with a great aunt of hers who is almost helpless. The old lady won't come down to New York and stay with us. She's rooted fast to that little Maine village. She took care of my wife's mother when she was a girl and made such a home for her as few orphan children have. Leroy's grandmother was left alone early in life. She had Mary (Mrs. Ellerton) promise never to neglect any wish of Aunt Prudence's, and it is the old lady's wish that Mary should take care of her in her last days. She seems to be one of those little Yankee women whose last days do last. I am glad that Mary can be with her, although it would simplify matters mightily if Aunt Prudence would only let us take care of her here. However, she is as averse to coming to the city as Leroy is to leaving it, so you can see my family dilemma has a couple of horns to be dealt with.

I haven't told Roy who you are. I am just letting him go to strangers in a way, so he will learn something, if it's in him to learn, and not be prejudiced by any obligations to our feelings. I believe it's in him, too. With best wishes to you and the children, I am

Yours as always,

JOHN ELLERTON

*Letter from DANIEL BRONSON
to JOHN ELLERTON*

TALTON, KANSAS, *March.*
DEAR JOHN:

Yours received. You know I'm glad to be able to return a small part of the obligation I owe to you. Send Leroy on at once. We can care for him nicely. I'm afraid he will find us dull company, but if he likes music, Eunice can play and sing some.

But business aside, Jack, it did me a world of good to see your hand-writing again and I jumped at the thought of having your boy with us. Took me back to the days when you and I came here together, you to get back your health, and I to make my fortune. We both succeeded, although you came through in one season, and I put in years at the job. I can see you now, white and delicate and brave in your suffering.

This land was desolate enough then. Only Hope filtered the atmosphere with a golden glamour. I've seen that glamour fade and the light turn to gloom more than once since the day I preëmpted my first hundred and sixty, and cut sod for my little dugout homestead. You know I built up on the swell above the river with not a claim-holder near me then. I can see three villages from the front porch now, and the Solomon Valley is like the Garden of Eden. And yet sometimes I am sentimental enough to wish for the old-time picture back again, the plain little house, the prairies rippling away in the distance, and the common loneliness, the common need for companionship. We were poor in those days, as property goes, but we were rich in the spirit of neighborly kindness. When our baby boy died, John Ellerton Bronson we called him, we could n't have endured it but for the loving sympathy of those homesteaders, poor as ourselves, but generous, and sympathetic in the sorrows of others.

I might have come into my own a little sooner in New York, but I 've always been glad I came West; glad that it was my privilege to see this valley change from a stretch of blossomy springtime prairie to a sweep of alfalfa bloom, from a seared waste of burned mid-summer grasses to the green acres of corn. It is worth the best years of one's life to have watched the transformation.

But I won't keep this up. Send Leroy out and we 'll fix that rheumatism.

My Seth is a perfect giant now. He finishes college next year. Carries football and track-meet honors enough to break down an ordinary constitution.

He has about made up his mind to go West when he gets through school. With us there is no real West, you know, till we get to the Rockies and beyond. Of course, I'd rather keep Seth here, and I need him. The ranch is getting to be more of a proposition to manage every year. We used to think we were busy, John, in the little corn patches and mowing lots up between the Vermont hills, before we went down to Yale. But when a bumper wheat crop comes our way out here, with four or five cuttings a season on the quarter section I have set to alfalfa, I can assure you that Satan must look to something else beside idle hands to get in his work in a Kansas summer. So I could give Seth a fine start in life, if he only took to the soil. But he doesn't. Since he was a little boy he has been crazy over mines and metals. He's an expert even now in those lines and can hardly wait to finish school, he is so eager for the West and the mountains and mining.

As I said, Eunice can play and sing some. She has finished with her teachers here and wants to go East in the Fall. I may ask your protection for her then. It was her mother's wish that she should have the opportunity for a musical career. Poor Ellen never really felt at home in Kansas. You know she was young when she died. It was only the hard work of a pioneer farmer's wife that fell to her lot, and when times grew better and we began to know some of the luxuries of the country, she was taken from us. I feel that that is the reason she was so eager to have our daughter given a musical education. She thought Eunice's life in Kansas would be as hers had been. John, I can't blame her. It was the women who bore the heaviest burdens here in the first years.

I shall miss my little girl dreadfully if she does go away. But we must not stand in the way of our children doing the best with their talents. And as you say, we can't keep them with us always. They must fly their own gait.

Again, I assure you we'll welcome your boy and do our best for his comfort.

With kind regards to Mrs. Ellerton, I am,

                    Faithfully yours,

                              DAN'L BRONSON

APRIL

Letter from *LEROY ELLERTON* to *HIS FATHER*

TALTON, KANSAS, *April*.

DEAR FATHER:

At last I am at the end of my journey, aching in every joint I ever had and some new ones I 've just discovered. But here I am in this God-forsaken Kansas region called the Solomon Valley. It may be a degree better than Death's Valley, which is still farther West somewhere, I am told. But since I am here, like Hamlet's ghostly father, "doomed for a certain time to walk this particular piece of earth," here for the first time, and I hope to Jiminy, the last as well, I 'll try to make the best of it if it kills me. But it does seem to me that I might have gone to Europe, like a gentleman, if you had n't come down on me with the ukase—"Go to the Solomon Valley for six months and come back cured forever."

Six months! I 'll be cured long before that, for I 'll be dead. I know, of course, that Indians and buffaloes, and maybe, cowboys are not to be found here now, but it is a cursed crude place to thrust an Eastern chap into. And

I don't mind saying, Father mine, that
I stand up for the prayers of the con-
gregation.

A drummer whom I met on the train
going out of Kansas City promised me
if I stayed here six months, there'd be
no pulling me out of Kansas again. Do
I look like that, I wonder. I can't see
where the valley comes in here. It is
as flat as a pancake for ten thousand
miles in every direction. I'm sure the
drainage is bad. Fine place to cure
rheumatism, though! Why my father
should think I'd ever get well in such
a miserable place, I can't comprehend.
It's the very bottom of the universe.
It's the under-side of the world.

When the Kansas City drummer left
the train at some little town, he said:
"You are new to the West. There is
a lot more for a rustic New Yorker to
learn out here than for a woolly Westerner to learn in the East. Some of
your folks learn quickly. Some are
slow, but when they do get their lesson,
they are the best fellows on earth. My
friend, I hope you may not only lose
your rheumatism out on the prairies, I
hope that you may also lose the notion
that this part of the Lord's earth, people and all, just happened, and wasn't
set down in the divine plan."

I hope he knows. But, to be honest,
there is something — I don't know
what — that seems restful after that

long car-ride. And it was long. I claim
I'm not a provincial, but I didn't know
that the world was quite so big both
ways. There is a tone in the air and
a little haze of pink on the orchards and
a thousand shades of green on the
landscape—all of which was pleasant
when I stepped off the Pullman at
Talton.

Your friend, Bronson, met me at the
station. He is a tall man, broad-
chested, erect, with grizzled dark hair
and bright dark eyes. He is a farmer,
of course, tanned face and hands, home
laundered shirt, plain clothes, and
freshly blacked boots—everything
showing the country-man in his "other
clothes."

"Is this Leroy Ellerton?" he asked.
And I must say it was a good voice to
hear. Something in its intonation was
in keeping with his strong face and stal-
wart form. His handshake, too, is
worth while. There is a kind of life in
his touch that thrills my nerves to the
shoulder. He had my suitcases and
me all stowed into a low, easy phaeton
before I knew it. I think that, for a
Westerner, he knows how to handle a
fellow with rheumatism. I hoped he
wouldn't try to talk to me nor make me
talk, and he didn't. If he'll always
anticipate my wishes, I can stand him,
I believe. In fact, it was I who made
him talk to me, like this:

"You knew my father, Mr. Bronson?" I asked him.

"Oh, yes; we came West together."

"You did? Why, I didn't know you had ever been East."

"I haven't, for a long time."

"You met my father in the East?" I asked. You see, Papa, I was getting interested in spite of myself.

"Yes," he said, "We were boys together."

"Father was just out of Yale University when he came West," I said, a little boastfully. Thought he might as well know whose son he had the honor of having for his guest. "He wrote you I was coming?"

The old fellow smiled a little. Then he said, "Yes, I had a letter from him and I came up to meet you."

And here I am settled in my room. The Bronsons have a better house than I had expected, and my den here is spotlessly clean. I've a big easy rocker that is very comfortable, and a mirror and a writing table. The view from my window is really wonderful. I'd no idea one could see so far except on the ocean. There is a stretch of the Solomon River in sight, and just now when the sun went down there was a kaleidoscope of blending colors in the sky.

I caught sight of a piano as I passed by the parlor door on my way to supper. I had supposed a parlor organ would be a luxury here. I reckon I'm doomed to listen to the daughter of the house play "Silver Threads among the Gold," and "Lambs of the Upper Fold"—oh, Father, what made you do it? But no matter. There isn't any Mrs. Bronson now, it seems, and this daughter is the housekeeper. She isn't unattractive, and she has a voice, magnetic and resonant like her father's, but soft and clear. She is a good cook. Her supper was a dream. And would you believe it, they had blue china and real silver. For the first, I suppose. To-morrow it will be a red table cloth and iron-stone china and soda biscuit, like we found up in York State farm houses last Summer. Oh, dear! Will this six months ever, ever end? Good-night, Father, I'm going to bed. If only I could sleep six months! I'll write to mother in the morning. And you may send this on to her as soon as you have read it. It will save my fingers some work. I'm glad she doesn't have to bring Aunt Prudence out here. * * * Seems to me the architect who built this Solomon Valley wasn't an expert in his line. The joke is on Solomon.

Yours with the back-ache,

Roy

Letter from **LEROY ELLERTON**
to **HIS MOTHER**

TALTON, KANSAS, *April.*

*In the south upper veranda,
with sunshine and no wind.*

DEAR MUMMY MINE:

My love and respects to Aunt Prudence—now that's my whole duty. She boxed my ears too often when I was a boy for me to do more than that for her. Not that the boxing wasn't good for me. I respect her for it now. But please consider that this sentence stands at the head of every letter that I write to you. Or I could have it embossed and framed to hang over her bed. Yes, yes, I'll keep still; I know her story. She was a mother to my grandmother, and a dear good *great*-mother (is that the way to put it?) to you, and you are awfully thankful that you can be with her. Seems to me the Ellertons have a lot to thank Providence for. You for being anchored in the dizzy social whirl of East Machias and your son and heir nesting out in the flat green Sahara thing called the Solomon Valley. For it's a very desert in length and loneliness and eternal sameness, but it is green as the greenest sheltered meadow of Maine

in mid-summer. And you say Aunt
Prudence has n't the rheumatism. Of
course not. I 've got all of it that 's
coming to this family. And anyhow,
she 'd not be over eighty and "all her
faculties bright" down in East Machias
if she had this plague of plagues. She 'd
be under a "sacred to the memory"
sign in the same form as John Brown's
body (Kansas John, you know), long
enough before eighty.

But I did n't mean to send this kind
of a letter. Father will forward to you
what I write to him. That will tell the
important things. I write with you in
mind, or I 'd never tell him some things.
Dear old Dad, I'd like to disinherit him
right now. But I said I 'd quit. Well,
I am Here. That is to say — Nowhere. Got here as per schedule.
See Papa's letter. Do you know this
Bronson outfit? That last is a Wild
West novel word. There is a Father
— not bad to look at for a farmer, but
all farmer. And there is a Son — I am
told. He is to appear in a later act of
this Wild West Show. And there is a
Daughter. All very interesting, no
doubt, if I was n't compelled to see them
daily. But they are not bad looking.
Eunice, that 's the girl, is not like a
farmer's daughter exactly, although I
tried at supper and breakfast to let her
go at that. She let me go, all right.
When I was n't thinking of this pain in

my shoulder, I couldn't help noticing her a little.

What does she look like, you will ask, because you are a woman. Frankly, I don't know. Just like any other green Kansas girl, I reckon. A little while ago, she came into my room and told me where to find this place at the south end of the upper hall. It is the coziest spot for a rheum — I mean, fellow. Cushions and a big easy chair and a willow couch. It's all screened in from mosquitoes and flies, and a perfect surge of sunshine rolls into it. There is a little table by the couch and a rug on the floor. I wonder if they didn't borrow a lot of these things from all the neighbors in town. Sets some folks up to have a New Yorker with them, you know.

However, the Bronsons don't act set up. They take me as a matter of course. When Eunice brought me out here, she said:

"This is to be your corner as long as you care for it. The sharp air is shut away by the gable and the south breeze is pleasant here in the hot weather. I hope it will be comfortable for you."

She was arranging the cushions, and as she shook up the pillows, I noticed her hands were smooth and her bare elbows actually had dimples. I was going to say some flattering nothings such as country girls feed on, but when

I looked into her face — I decided not to do it. Still, I am afraid I'll be expected to do the gallant thing by this Eunice. Mother, rheumatism and gallantry don't go together, and I don't know why I must spend energy on this daughter. I was sent here and I'm serving out a six months' sentence, that's all.

Though for your comfort, Mummy, I will tell you that the Bronsons don't seem to expect much of me yet. How it will be on a longer acquaintance, I can't say, nor what I'll do when they begin to flock to New York to pay back this visit. Good-bye now. This and Dad's letter will tell all I know. It's a warm, drowsy cove up in this corner of my cell — all Kansas is a cell to me. And I'm going to sleep as many hours as I can. Don't let Aunt Prudence wear you all away.

Affectionately,

ROY

MAY

Letter from LEROY ELLERTON to HIS FATHER

TALTON, KANSAS, *May.*

MY DEAR FATHER:

I meant to write you several days ago, but we've been so busy, I put it off. You'll wonder what I could find to make me busy—I who have been leaning on cushions for so long. Well, everybody out here is that way. And since I've been idle for a year, it seems good to be at work again. I've been here six weeks. I didn't think I could get rid of so much pain in so short a time. This is a wonderful air. Why, I sleep all night now, and I could eat anything from a cucumber pickle to a Kansas politician. The Bronsons are really well-bred people, even if they do live in Kansas, and they keep the neatest home and set up the best table—or is it I who am getting my old Yale appetite back?

We have had an abundance of rain this season, and it is the greenest world out here a poor city fellow with memories of brick walls and dust ever looked upon. If the fresh air fiends could only send their slum children this way they would get some of the real thing. You'd be surprised to know how many Eastern magazines find their way out

here. I was amazed when I saw the
number of books and the kind of books
in the bookcases. Why, Father, they
are just like New York in that, now
really they are. More so than in even
some swell homes. I know young ladies
in the East who read less, I do believe,
than Eunice does.

But I can't read all the time. So I
make myself useful about the house.
They have wads of flowers in bloom and
I keep the bouquets fresh in the vases.
Big business for a young man of
twenty-three! Also I play the piano for
Eunice. She sings very well, consider-
ing. And she plays for my solos in
better time than you'd think. You see,
Pappy dear, I want you to know that
these folks out here are n't such heathen
as you, living in New York and never
coming out of your shell, would think.

I believe I have n't mentioned the son,
Seth Bronson. He is a physical giant,
fair though, like Eunice. Did I tell
you that Eunice has a pretty fine skin
for Kansas? But this Seth,—well, he
does n't like me, I 'm sure. Although
he is a quiet fellow, I suspect he 's not
half the fool he might be taken for in
New York. He 's quiet like his father.
I was afraid he 'd bore me to death, but
instead he lets me alone pretty severely.

He has just come home for his vacation from some place called Manhattan.
(How homesick even the writing of

that name makes me!)   For a college
man it is surprising how he can drop
in among the hired men and work just
like one of them.   "How can a fellow
be a farm-hand and a college student?"
I asked him the other day.   He stared
at me a minute and said, "If you went
down to Manhattan, you'd think a fellow wouldn't want to be a farm-hand
unless he *was* a college student, — not
if he wanted to win out anyhow."

One rainy afternoon he asked me
up to his room for the first time.
Why, Father, it was a regular college
den, with pennants and baseball and
football trophies.   Seth is a champion
at these things, it seems, and a dozen
pictures and tokens in his room show
it.   And you ought to see the way he
can handle a horse!   Isn't any more
excited over the most fractious one than
I'd be over a cat.   I was out in the pas-
ture — a township big — when he caught
one last evening.   The whole drove
came at us like army cavalry.   You
know I got my first Yale "Y" in a pole
vault.   I'd have vaulted over a nine-
foot hedge fence just then, if I'd only
had the pole.   You can't do that on a
last year's sunflower stalk, and that was
the longest timber in sight.   Seth never
stopped whistling, and only looked side-
ways after the colt he wanted.   Had it,
too, before I knew what to do next.
That horse catch awakened a sleeping

force in me. I forgot my rheumatism
altogether and stood straighter than I
have in a year. I do believe that somewhere back in a previous incarnation I
was something of a centaur myself, that
I somehow belonged to the soil and
planted and harvested and was at home
on horseback. I feel it in some new
pulse-beat of my blood. Anyhow,
rheumatism or no rheumatism, I'm
going to be riding and driving and
catching loose horses too, before Fall.
I know I can do it as well as that six-
footer with his two hundred pounds
gross on the scales. The lubber!

Eunice is a musical graduate from
some college out here they call Washburn. They talk a lot about it and she
and Seth are forever guying each other
about the merits of their two schools.
That's one good trait of this family.
They have some sense of humor and
can see a joke clear across the Solomon
to the far prairie. Her room is oppo-
site mine, and the door is always open
in the daytime. That room is all one
symphony of Yale blue; only its white
"W" for Washburn marks the differ-
ence between it and the blue of my own
Yale den at home. I spoke to Eunice
about it one day and she said something
about the founder, Ichabod Washburn,
being a product of Yale. But it didn't
seem clear to me.

Of course, I told them all about your

wonderful career at Yale and how only
one other member of your class ever
out-ranked you — I've forgotten that
fellow's name long ago — how it was
always neck and neck between you two.
Father Bronson's eyes glistened with
real tears as I told the old stories you
used to tell me of your college days and
of this old chum of yours. Poor old
Bronson! I suppose he never had a
chance at a thing like that in his younger
years. But no matter, Father, it is really
surprising how much of a gentleman
even a farmer like Bronson can be. He
is one of the most sincere and well-
meaning men I have ever known. He
is even beginning to dignify farming in
my eyes. And Eunice is just like him.
But Seth — well, there was a kind of
odd smile on his face when I talked of
you. Jealousy, I suppose, on account
of his father. These poor Kansas fellows can't help it.

I must quit now and write to mother.
Her last letter says Aunt Prudence is
getting stronger every day, but she adds
that the old lady is more than ever de-
termined not to let her out of sight,
which means a summer of it for Madam
Ellerton, I suppose. She says she gets
the letters I send to you the next mail
after you read them. Good Papa!
Good-bye, I'm doing fine.

LEROY

Letter from **LEROY ELLERTON**
to **HIS MOTHER**

Talton, Kansas, *May.*

Dear Mother Mine:

This is your dutiful "loved and only"
who is writing to you this exquisite May
morning. While you are shivering before a wood fire down at the beginning
of things in East Machias where Maine
starts in to grow a United States, out
here in the heart of nowhere, watered
by the Solomon River, there is a
boundless vasty world of sunshine running loose. And while you are still
clinging to your long-sleeved flannels
and keeping screened away from
draughts, I am sitting on the broad
northeast veranda, letting the wind,
soft but full of tone, pour over me like
the surf at Coney Island, and I'm only
a little more decently clad than a surf
bather, too, for I have all my summer
regimentals on now. It is early Summer here,—if only my pen could make
you feel its balmy breath! Quite a poet
I'm getting to be. Didn't know it was
in me before. But they say Kansas
will develop whatever tendency to
crankism is in one's constitution. Mine
seems to be a sickish sentimentalism.
But it is only to you, Mother, that

I mean to let it reveal itself, although
Dad is such a good fellow, I do turn
loose to him now and then. But you
were always my safety valve, Mother,
and I should have blown up long ago
without you.

You don't know how glad I am to
hear from you, for you can understand
me better than Dad can. Blessed old
Hard Shell writes the funniest letters
to me. Seems to think I 'll die of home-
sickness. I may yet, but *he* can't hit
my homesick streak. I 'm not quite the
martyr he takes me for. I 'm *beginning* to get settled. Why, Mummy
dear, Kansas is on the map, and trains
run *to* New York as well as away from
it. John Ellerton did n't kick me clear
off the universe when he shoved me over
the Alleghany ridge. I 'll tell him so
sometime when my rheumatism is
better.

But back to your letter. I 'm glad
you are so contented on that stern and
rock-bound upheaval above sea level.
You say that after all you are never unhappy up in Maine because you love the
villages and country ways and byways.
Maybe I have inherited some streak of
that thing myself, for I am getting
wonderfully acclimated out here — getting accustomed to the openness of this
valley. It is *open,* too. No use to get
behind a ladder to change your neck-tie,
as we used to say, for there are too many

folks on the other side of the ladder.
Yet all sides of the ladder interest me
and keep on doing it.

I must tell you about Eunice. She is
not like any other farmer's girl I ever
saw. There's a cute little curve at the
corners of her mouth that saves it from
being too set. She's got a mind of her
own; says she'd vote if she lived in a big
city in Kansas where women can do
that. But she says it so matter-of-fact
like and all, that I believe she would
do it gracefully and not be undigni-
fied if she wanted to. She does everything else that way, even if she does live
in this Wild West. But she is wrapped
up in her music, is just crazy about it,
and wants to go on studying it somewhere. All the Bronsons seem set
enough in their notions.

Kansas seems to put purpose into
everybody. I confess, Mother, it makes
me ashamed of myself sometimes. I
don't seem ever to have had a motive
for living. New York just supplied my
outside life. Inside of me, I've not begun to live yet.

Seth, the big son of the home, is
bound to go West and make a mining
expert of himself; seems to know the
layers of earth clear down to where they
spell places with dashes instead of letters. (Awful Leroy! he won't say that
any more.)

But why can't he stay here, where

he's needed? I'd stay with my father—
if he'd only let me. He's thrust me out
into a cold, cold world. But it's a sun-
shiny world this time, and Solomon in
all his glory was never arrayed as this
Solomon Valley is in the grandeur of
this May morning. Not that this is any
finer than New England or York State.
There's just such an eternal lot more
of it to be seen all at once, it makes a
fellow catch his breath—and dimly
from somewhere comes up that old saying, "eye hath not seen," etc. Not
many such places for the eye to see, I'm
sure of that. * * *

Those stars stand for the auto honks.
Think of it! I just saved myself from
total ruin the week after I came here. I
had started in one evening to enlarge
on the delights of motoring. It had
been raining for an endless time and I
was a dark dead blue. So I had to brag
about myself or swear. The sunset had
just rebuilt the world, made a new
heaven and a new earth all out of old
gray rags of clouds and a mud-sodden
land, and a free sweep of warm wind
was cleaning house for all out-of-doors.
Well, I'd just begun to brag about
some motoring I'd done in my ancient
Eastern life, when Father Bronson said:

"Eunice, you and Seth might take
Mr. Ellerton out to the hills with the
machine, this evening, if it is not too
damp."

I supposed he meant the sewing machine or mowing machine or the sulky plough. I'd not been as far as the barn then. But I had the grace to let up on motoring, — won't say about swearing, but that was under my breath, — while I resigned myself to my accursed fate. And in three minutes, if Seth didn't run out the spankingest big automobile — Well, I nearly fell off the front steps. And I've never said "motor" since. * * * There goes my call again.

Eunice is down by the front veranda, waiting to take me and this letter over to Talton. The R. F. Deliverer passed an hour ago. They really do have R. F. D.'s out here and mail *daily*. Good as East Machias about that. I can just see Eunice's hair and the back of her neck behind the vines as she sits in the auto. That dark blue linen suit and square sailor collar and the pile of silky hair above it look good to me. So good-bye, dearest of Mummies.

Lovingly,

LEROY

JUNE

Letter from *LEROY ELLERTON* to *HIS FATHER*

TALTON, KANSAS, *June.*

DEAR FATHER:

Here it is mid-June almost before we can think. I am *so much better* I take no note of time. The hours always drag when one is suffering, and they seem to fly when we forget ourselves. That's what I've been doing. I think I shouldn't have thought about the time at all if your last letter hadn't had so much of condolence about my being *shut up* out here. That's a good term for it, so we'll let it go at that.

I'm finding something new to do every day, and every day I am getting a new power of resistance. This must be the best of all seasons on these prairies. It quit raining back in May and there is a clear blue dome ten trillion miles across, sloping down to a level green earth that has no bound at all, but ravels out into a blur of pale lavender or deep purple where dome meets plain. Talk about Kansas cyclones! I've forgotten the sound of thunder.

"Who knows whither the clouds have fled?
In the unseared heavens they leave no wake,
And eyes forget the tears they have shed," —

And I have nearly forgotten my rheumatism.

The June days are warm here, but the nights are glorious, with always a ripple of soft air sweeping up from the south when the sun goes down. And such sunsets! Why, Poppy, they are gorgeous. Bronson's place is located with special regard for them, I guess. Eunice and I watched the show last night. If I were an artist I'd put this Solomon Valley on canvas a mile across. Up and down lie acre on acre of heavy green corn land, with golden wheat fields between, and sweeps of alfalfa -with its shimmering purple bloom— the most beautiful herbage that ever grew. And through it all winds the Solomon River, with its fringe of greenery. Beyond lie pastures with herds of cattle and hay fields brown and yellow with the mid-summer heat.

Across this spread of land the level rays of sunset fling their splendor, while far up the sky a radiant glory of color no artist can ever paint—well, that's the Solomon Valley. And stretching away to the very bound of the world, fold on fold, is a wavy richness of greens and browns and gold, with purple shadows into which it all melts at last, and the pink tinting overhead slowly softening into silvery cloud mist. It is worth a journey to see. You may not care for all this landscape. You would if you saw it as I do.

The Bronsons aren't half bad,
Father. Eunice is a fine girl, really.
She can sing very well — for Kansas,
and she rides still better. I couldn't get
very lonely with such a wide-awake girl
to keep me company. She is the joy of
her father's heart, although he is proud
of Seth. Seth is going on West to Ore-
gon, or somewhere else, as soon as he
gets through school. The young fellow
is silly about mining and can't see that
he ought to stay right here, that nothing
could be better for him. But that's just
the way with some fellows — never do
know what is good for them. Why, the
longer I stay here, the more I see what
the ranch should mean to one born to it.
Of course, it isn't like the office and all
that buying and selling and loaning and
foreclosing business you have ready for
me when I quit "doing time" out here.
Harvesting a thousand or so bushels of
wheat isn't done behind glass partitions
with onyx-panelled walls and roller-top
desks and glittering fixtures and with a
brick-and-mortar wall frowning before
every window. That's to be my setting
when I do business, while Seth here has
a range such as the wild cattle of the
plains once held, and the eternal swell
and slide of all the winds of heaven.
Why should he want to leave all this
and go "experting" down the black,
blinding alleys of coal or copper de-
posits under the crust of this beautiful
earth? Even I know better than that.

This farm life appeals to me more and
more.

But that's enough about Seth. It is
Eunice who interests me. She does sing
beautifully, and her one foolish notion —
just like Seth's going West — is to go
to New York and have her voice trained
and then to go abroad maybe, for more
training, and then to sing to crowded
houses. A career! What does a
woman — especially a Kansas woman
and a farmer's daughter at that — need
with one anyhow? And Eunice is a
Jayhawker, all right. I like to tease her
about the West, she is so loyal to her
State. I've ridiculed everything here
just to see how she'll fight for Kansas.
She is so handsome when she is a little
bit excited. Then her brown eyes are
full of fire and there is a pink flush on
her cheeks. She is fair, I told you, with
curly golden brown hair and the softest
big brown eyes.

Tuesday, Eunice said, "If you will
go with me to-morrow afternoon, I'll
show you something you'd never find
duplicated in your York State nor any
other little Atlantic seaboard reserva-
tion."

"What is that?" I asked.

"A forgotten bit of the sea," Eunice
answered.

Late the next afternoon, we were off
for a long spin to a little town miles
away, where she had an errand of some

sort. We had an early supper at the
hotel and then we took in the town with
its average number of uninteresting
things and one or two odd features such
as every little town possesses for its
own.

On our way home Eunice turned
from the main road to show me that forgotten bit of the sea she had promised.
It was a beautiful evening, with
such a sunset as I have described. And
Eunice — but no matter.

What we went out for to see was a
wonderful welling up of salt water just
like the clear green waves off Long
Island. A huge mound of earth thirty
feet high and a hundred across forms the
cup which the water fills to the brim.
The depth of this pool is only guessed
at. So here it lies, by long secret underground ways reaching out to the sea or
some salt spot a thousand miles away
maybe. Æons and æons ago the sea
waves swept over Kansas, I am told by
my geology. And then came its up-
heavals and down-settlings, its stand-
patting and boss-busting and machine-
ruling, and all the whole grand mix-up.
In which mix the sea went off and forgot
this little bit of it. Forgot the combina-
tion on the cut-off. Or maybe the
plumbing of this old earth was as de-
fective then as a New York flat is
to-day. Anyhow, this precious, clear,
green pool of salty water was forgot-

ten; and year on year, century on century, rising and falling like the tides of the ocean, it dimpled under the summer winds and smiled back at the skies above it. Like the pioneers of this Solomon Valley it defied the drouth to burn it out, or the winter blizzard to lock it up with ice. And the Indians came and called it Waconda — Spirit Water — and worshipped ever what they could not understand.

Eunice and I sat down beside this spring and saw the full moon swing up the eastern sky and flood the land with its chastened radiance. All the Solomon Valley lay like a dream of peace under its spell. If I live a thousand years, I'll never see another moonrise like that nor another such valley of rest and sweet dreamy quiet beauty, until the gates of Paradise swing out for me.

And, Father, nothing in that scene fitted so well as that Kansas girl, Eunice Bronson, in her pretty white dress, with the wild rose bloom on her cheek. Somehow the fever of the world slips off out here sometimes and we get down to the real worth of things, without so much of sham and show. But this letter is already miles too long, so good-night.

Aff. yours,

ROY

AUGUST

Letter from LEROY ELLERTON to HIS FATHER

TALTON, KANSAS, *August.*

DEAR FATHER:

I have neglected you too long, but you know when I *don't* write, I'm *all* right. I am getting better all the time, although I'm not quite well enough to go home yet. You see, Father dear, this is a whole lot better country than you know anything about back in New York. Of course, you were out here once. I don't wonder you lost your rheumatism. There is no place for it here. Why, right now New York must be like a bake oven. Oh, but I know how hot it is! Of course, it is hot here too, but it bakes out the rheumatism.

Your little note this morning brought good news. To think of Aunt Pru getting her grip on things again, forgetting her aches and pains, and bundling mother off to Europe for the rest of the season as a reward for caring for her! I guess the old lady is better-hearted, after all, than we give her credit for being. Glorious for Mummy, isn't it? And she deserves it ten times over. But to come back to things earthy — that's myself — you are wrong this

time. It didn't make me a bit unhappy that it wasn't I who was sailing
toward Europe. We can't do all we
want to do, of course. It's much ado
with some of us to do what we ought.
There's Seth Bronson with his nose
underground smelling out rock forma-
tions, when the call of the soil ought to
be music to him. I can picture every
day what a fellow could do with Seth's
opportunity here. I think sometimes
he half envies me what's coming to me
soon—the city pavement and sky-
scraper structures, and the jostling
human herd roaring down those gloomy
cracks that cities call streets. There
are no scrapers out here. The sky is
too everlasting far up. And only the
great hand of God Almighty can fling
the little cirri cloud flakes in groups
that slope toward the zenith, or pile the
black stupendous thunder folds against
the western horizon and illumine them
through and through with electric
splendor, the token of His own glory.
I never saw much of that from
your office windows at home. The
great lack with city-reared children,
I've figured out, is that we never see
anything but the work of men's hands.
The grandest structures we may watch
go up from a hole in the ground. All
the shipping and ship-building is swung
by machinery and some man is at the

crane's end guiding the pulleys.
And every pretty park and bit of
natural beauty has the water-works
back of it and some sooty fellow in the
engine room controlling it all. He can
give and take away, can make a world
of blue grass and blossoms, or — turn
off the power — and leave only burr-
grown sand. It takes the great forests
or a stretch of prairie land, something
only the Big Architect can build, to put
a little reality into a fellow's mind, and
anchor him to something permanent.
Maybe, Daddy, you have said some of
this to me before, but it did n't stick till
I worked it out myself here. This is n't
a Robinson Crusoe island. I don't go
any on the hermit stunt. Neither
is it "the madding crowd's ignoble
strife" and strut. It is the peace half
way between the two, and Seth Bronson
is an idiot, that 's all. He can't hear the
message of every growing stalk of
wheat, and the music of mowing ma-
chines, and know the freedom from the
crazy crowd forever at his heels. One's
work counts on the farm with Nature
for a perpetual partner, putting up the
big share of the capital, and with time
now and then to stop and live, while the
eternal wrangle of men and man-made
things goes scrambling and screaming
on in the congested centres of human
population. Green as I am, I know this

much, and I say again that Seth is an idiot — fifty-seven varieties of an idiot, and I begrudge the ink it takes to dot the *i* when I write his title. He may go to * * * the stars. That isn't profanity. And I'll write about better subjects.

I must tell you, Daddy, what a glorious jaunt we had this week. I've teased Eunice about the little shrubs they call trees out here. I've told her over and over about the real forests up in York State, while she has been saying all Summer,

"Wait till August, and we will go to see some real trees, grand old oaks."

I asked her if they were of this Spring's planting, and would be ripe in August.

But she would only say — "Wait and see."

We are having long and clear days. The sky is all fine gold and the earth is a shading from yellow green to the deepest brown. This thin air just suits me and the nights have that dry soft breath that cools but never chills. Let me see, was it Leroy Ellerton who used to dread the damp night air on account of the rheumatism?

But about the trees. Eunice and I had gone miles and miles up the Solomon Valley for a long picnic day. And, Father, we did see such a grove of beau-

tiful oaks as you'd never think a flat old
prairie could grow. They were tucked
away in a little valley, where a muddy
creek comes winding down to the Solomon River. You could hardly guess,
unless you followed the stream, what
was hidden in that deep valley. The
dip and swell of the prairie showed us
only a line of green leafiness, until sud-
denly we were at the gateway of a grove
sheltering a summer assembly camp-
ground.

Nestling under the shadows of the
oaks were tents and tents, the out-door
homes of the folk all round about this
region, who come here every August-
time. They were good to look at, too,
these inhabitants of the Plains, for, to
be square with you, Father, these folks
are so much more worth while than I
ever thought could be out here that I'm
going to be honest enough to say so. Of
course, there are none of them quite like
Eunice, but that's another story. The
earth is the Lord's here, all right, but the
fulness thereof is piling up in the banks
in little towns like Talton. Friends
of the Bronsons that I met at this
Chautauqua affair do very much like
real Easterners; they send their children to college, and they don't seem to
think much about it if some member of
the family goes to Europe for a summer
vacation. I've not done that yet, you

may recall. Say, Dad, if you know of
any young city chap who wants to go
where he can patronize the benighted
community by his presence, don't send
him this way, please. When Eunice's
friends spoke in that commonplace fashion about going abroad, all I could say
was that, "Mother is travelling in
Switzerland now," or, "My father's
business takes him over often." Re-
flected glory beats no glory at all, and
I just couldn't meet all those friends
of the Bronsons as a provincial, even a
New York provincial.

There were many interesting things
that day for me, but what struck me
most forcibly was the law-abiding spirit
of the crowd in that assembly park. It
was no beer-garden set. Why, I can't
bear the thought of some of our resorts,
now that I suppose I'll be seeing them
soon. * * *

All this before I get to the trees.
Ages ago, dense forests must have cov-
ered this region, which some force later
reduced to a grass land, and the prairie
fires kept it thus. Only this winding
creek had crept lovingly about these
great oak trees — encircling them penin-
sular fashion, shielding them from the
flames. Through long sunny days and
soft dark nights in years that rolled up
centuries, the beautiful trees grew and
spread their branches. Deep through

the black earth they struck strong roots
that held firm in the day of the cyclone's
wrath.   They must be very old; they
were growing here, I'm sure, when the
Pilgrims set foot on Plymouth Rock.
And earlier, too, when Coronado and
his Spanish knights wandered up to the
Smoky Hill River country in search of
Quivira and its fabled gold-paved cities.
They are fine and venerable looking
enough to have been lifting their young
green boughs to the rains and bending
against the hot winds when Columbus
sighted land that October morning four
hundred years ago.

You may think I'm getting poetical.
It is in the air out here.   I tell you,
Father, there's nothing new and crude
about this Solomon Valley.   It is old
and time-seasoned.

That was a glorious day we spent under the oaks, with their grand green
heads and their hundred-foot spread of
shade.   I've heard you talk about your
boyhood up in Vermont enough to know
how you would feel in such a place for
one long, lazy August day.   On the way
back to Bronsons, we talked about the
old oak trees and the different things
they mean to different minds.   One of the
Yale men used to tell us, in his classes,
how we made the world each for himself, and how we must each read out
and then act out his own destiny.   It

all came back to me in that homeward
ride, as many another long-forgotten
lesson will come sometimes.

We didn't do any record-breaking
speeding that evening. It was too good
to live slowly. The Solomon Valley is
in its late summer grandeur, and with
the purple mist of evening hanging over
it, the whole thing slipped from a wide
landscape through a soft blur of helio-
trope twilight into a black velvety night.
Eunice is artistic enough to see all this.
She is not like Seth. While he is peer-
ing underground, her head is among the
stars. She has her dream of a musical
career cut and basted and fitted on.
I've found that out, all right. Coming
home we turned aside again to visit that
spring, the one the Indians called Waconda. Whatever it may have meant
to them, it had a message for me. The
hour was that dim, shadowy time

> "*When all the jarring notes of life*
> *Seem blending in a psalm,*
> *And all the angles of the strife*
> *Slow rounding into calm.*"

The sharp edges of the day are soft-
ened and the world is made of curves
and harmonious tones of color, pink and
gray and amethyst. Looking out toward the Solomon River winding by
black shadowed corn fields and gray-
green meadows, I pictured the day when
the red man ruled here and this pool of

salt sea water was his shrine. His dead
lay buried in the bottom lands by the
slow-moving Solomon and he stood
on this huge mound and sung his weird
death-songs, and made offerings of beads
and arrows and trophies to the waters,
that the Spirit of the Waters would be
kind to his departed ones. Did he lift
his face in hope to the wide heavens
above him and did he hear in the wan-
dering winds, that ebb and swell
across the plains, a voice that spoke of
peace and the Great Chieftain's promise
of a future life?

And then I thought farther back to
the day when the sea had left this bit
of itself, one lonely gem of emerald
waters, upon the desert plains. And I
thought how down the years, through a
hundred hundred generations of men
it had kept its place, with all the sea's
traditions, color, taste, and motion, rising and falling regularly like the ocean
tides, here in the heart of the great
green plains, a thousand miles from any
ocean waters. And I told myself a
reason for it all. The mystery of
Waconda and its world-old, world-wide
lesson came to me like a revelation. I
wondered what it meant to Eunice. We
had read the same story in the old oak
trees. When I spoke to her of the red
man, and the origin of the spring, she
said:

"We have another notion of the Indians out here, but I, too, love this place which they must have loved. Waconda has a story for me, a mystery I have never yet fathomed. I wonder why it is here so far from the great sea, to which it belongs, and if it does not yearn, after the manner of inanimate things, for the great heaving ocean of which it could be a part.

"I can understand it better, maybe, because I, too, am held here in this valley by ties hard to break, when all the time I am yearning to get out into the world, to study and work, and then, as a singer, to give delight to lovers of song."

I wanted to tell her the message the waters were bringing to me. But it wasn't the time then. She is so set on this notion of a musical career.

"We can never see with other people's eyes in this world," she said when we stood up for a last look at the valley, all tenderly gray, deepening into purple. "Waconda tells you one story and me another, and they may be very different. If you should ask Seth, he would give you a mineral analysis, slick and comprehensive. To Father, it is a tragedy. He was too near to the time when this soil was red with the martyr blood of the first white settlers. I am glad we are a generation away from all that, and can look beyond it to the mystery of old Waconda of the long, long ago."

All the way home, Eunice sàng sweet ballads, Indian love songs, and snatches from an Arapahoe melody:

" Waconda, hear us, hear us!
Waconda, Oh, behold us!
Like the embers dying, O Waconda!
Like the pale mist flying, O Wa-
conda!
Wood and prairie fade before us,
Hills and streams our Fathers gave
us,
Home, and friends of home, O Wa-
conda!
And thy children roam, O Waconda!
Like the weary winds, homeless cry-
ing."

Her voice is beautiful, but it seems to fit these open spaces more than it would the crowded, hemmed-in opera houses. That's her business, though, not mine.

Good-night. There's a lot of doings planned ahead and I must get my beauty sleep.

Affectionately,

ROY

SEPTEMBER

Letter from JOHN ELLERTON to DANIEL BRONSON

NEW YORK CITY, *September.*
MY DEAR OLD DAN:

Roy's case is very hopeful. Why, he's a credit to me; learns faster than I thought he could; writes like he had to instruct his green old father concerning the merits of your family. You must be a splendid teacher. The joke is on the cub, of course. He's got as bad a case of Kansas fever as he had of New York rheumatism. Now, watch him squirm when I write to him to come home.

You have carried him over the slough as you used to carry me when I was helpless with rheumatism, you blessed old son of a horse thief. Just as you carried me over the rough places at Yale.

Yours,

JOHN ELLERTON

P. S. Mrs. Ellerton is in Europe now. Will spend the Winter on the Continent.

Letter from JOHN ELLERTON to HIS SON LEROY

NEW YORK, *September.*

DEAR ROY:

Your six months is nearly up, — only two weeks more. On your own confession your rheumatism left you in August, but I wanted you to be sure of it. You must be very tired of the Bronson outfit by this time, so I write to tell you to come home at once. I sail for Liverpool the sixteenth. Come as soon as you get this, and we can go together. You might spend the Fall in Italy with your mother. That would just suit you. You need n't answer. Come.

Your loving father,

JOHN ELLERTON

Letter from LEROY ELLERTON
to HIS FATHER

Talton, Kansas, *September.*
Dear Daddy:

What's the blooming matter with you,
anyhow? And why did you ever think
I'd want to spend a glorious Autumn
in such a Dago land as Italy? I haven't
asked for a reprieve, have I? I'm willing to serve out my sentence here. You
have gone galumphing off to Liverpool
a dozen times without me; and mother
has been in Maine in the Summers or
in Florida in the Winters, leaving me
an orphan, since I was sixteen. Kansas
is just in its glory now. They say the
Octobers are splendid here. I can believe it, and I'm writing to ask for an
extension of my sentence of six months,
on account of bad behavior.

You know I came West under pro-
test. Now, why do you insist on cutting
off two weeks of the time just when this
old earth is at its finest? You can't
know in smoky, noisy, rushing New
York, where the sun, moon, and stars,
the changing seasons, and everything
beautiful is lost in the crazy, reeling
masses of people and mountains of brick
walls, — you can't know what this time
of the year is like out here.

" All the rich and gorgeous glintings
Merging into matchless tintings,
As the summer blossoms dwindle,
And the autumn landscapes kindle,
Setting vale and upland flaming
In a glory past all naming."

That's the Solomon Valley in October, and a myriad changing hues make the landscape radiant with beauty. Everything is arranged for three or four weeks ahead. When you see mother, tell her I'm the best I've been in three years. I've got the recuperative power of Aunt Pru.

When I read your letter to Eunice she looked a little disappointed, I thought, but when I told her I should ask for a stay of execution she only laughed and recommended me to Italy. Mr. Bronson is waiting to take this letter to Talton. Hope you will have a fair voyage to Liverpool, but I can't possibly join you now.

Yours,

ROY

Special Delivery Letter from JOHN ELLERTON to HIS SON

NEW YORK, *September.*

DEAR ROY:

I have put off sailing until the twenty-first, so you can get here in time to go with me. Now don't think your father too blind not to see that you are merely frittering away your time with a green young Kansas girl. You are born and bred to the city and you went out to that God-forsaken Solomon Valley only to get rid of your rheumatism. Now that it is gone, you must begin the life of a New York business man in real earnest. You can spend the Fall in Italy. That is your final polish. Then the grind begins for you. I need you in my office now and as soon as we get home from this trip abroad, you and I will make a firm that will cut rock in this great, busy, rushing city. Don't write, but come.

Your loving father,

J. E.

*Special Delivery Letter from LEROY
ELLERTON to HIS FATHER*

TALTON, KANSAS, *September.*

DEAR FATHER:

Your "special" got here all right. I
had my plans all set for another month,
but I am obedient, if I'm anything. It
is too late for me to make the twenty-
first. I'll follow on the next steamer. I
told Eunice last night what you said
about my staying in New York. You
need not be uneasy about that. She is as
willing I should be in that big human
maelstrom as you are eager to fasten
me there. I found that out without her
knowing it. I had thought—but never
mind. I didn't tell her what you wrote
about her being a "green Kansas girl."
I'll write you at Liverpool and join you
there later.

Yours,

ROY

Telegram

LEROY ELLERTON,
    TALTON, KANSAS.

I sail the twenty-fourth. Come at once.

J. E.

Telegram

JOHN ELLERTON,
    NEW YORK CITY.

Can't make it.

ROY

NOVEMBER

*Letter from JOHN ELLERTON to
DANIEL BRONSON*

LIVERPOOL

DANIEL BRONSON,
TALTON, KANSAS, U. S. A.
DEAR DAN:

I can't tell you how I regret missing your letter which Leroy sent on to me here.

Had I received it sooner, I could have cabled Roy to stay in New York until after your daughter Eunice should arrive. He could have made her feel at home at once.

You see, I had to come on here without Roy, and when he reached New York from the West, a cablegram from me kept him from sailing at once. I had to leave some business for him to look after. I had already wired for him to come on before I received the letter of yours asking me to look after Miss Eunice. And he will be on the ocean when she reaches the city. But I have sent word to friends of ours who will meet her and do all any one could do for her, I am sure, except possibly Mrs. Ellerton, if she were at home. She and Roy will spend the next two months in Italy.

After all you did for Roy, this is a poor return to you and Miss Eunice, and you know how sincerely I regret it. I hope your daughter may like the city as well as Roy seemed to like Kansas last Summer. I haven't seen him yet, but look for him on the next steamer.

Yours faithfully,

JOHN ELLERTON

P. S. We will all be back in March or April and if we don't show Eunice a good time, it will be the fault of New York, not of the Ellerton family.

*Letter from EUNICE BRONSON,
New York, to DANIEL BRON-
SON, Kansas.*

NEW YORK, *November.*
MY DEAR FATHER:

I reached N. Y. all right and found
friends of the Ellertons waiting for me,
who took me to the Conservatory of
Music at once. I am nicely settled and
I know I shall be as happy here as I
can be anywhere away from you. The
home on the Solomon seems pretty
good to me to-night. I am homesick
for Kansas for a minute. But only for
a minute. The teachers here are
full of praise for my work, and the
promise of my future. Oh, if I could
only fill a great opera house with my
song until the very rafters rang with
applause! I hope my ambition isn't
sinful, because I know I should be giving the sweetest pleasure to music-hun-
gry hearts. And why should not my
ambition be fulfilled, if I put all my
strength into my work? Since I was
just a slip of a girl, I have been looking
forward to this day when I should have
the opportunity to try my powers.
Even in the time when coming East to
study seemed a wild impossibility for a
Kansas girl, because we hadn't the
money then, and New York was such a
far-away thing, frowning coldly on a

farmer's daughter from the West. But
now, oh, Father, I'm walking on the
cloud-tops, I'm so happy to be here in
this whirl of real life. If it wasn't for
you and Seth I'd forget there ever was
a Solomon Valley.

It is so good of you, Father dear, to
let me come, when the house must be
lonely, with only a housekeeper in it.
You realize, for you have lived here, how
great it is for me to get away from the
farm and the narrow life on the prairie,
and to be in this wonderful city where
they *do things*. Buy to-day, and sell to-
morrow; not plant in September — and
maybe — after a long Winter and
longer Spring, late in June garner in
the harvest as we do our wheat. Pro-
vided always that the drouth and the
winds and the fly — and the May floods
— have been merciful.

I can see your eyes twinkle as you
say:

"It is good wheat money that is sending my daughter to New York."

It isn't wheat money that keeps this
city on the everlasting jump, I am sure,
and the queer thing in all this to me is
that I seem to feel at home in it. I do
believe that somewhere back in some
past incarnation that Theosophists understand (I don't), I do believe that
I was a real city girl, born and bred.
Of course, I'm a Jayhawker still, but
it is just glorious here. I know I'm

coming into my own, into freedom and
opportunity, into the busy pulsing life
of the great tides of humanity that
surge these streets as the waters of the
Atlantic surge up against its shores.
And I am a part of it all, instead of
being tied to the prairie like poor lonely
little Waconda Springs, lost and forgotten by the big ocean to which it belongs.

And Seth is gone too. The call of
the West was as strong for him as the
call of the East for me. He has sent
me a perfectly grand letter from the
Columbia River country. No use talking, Father, one or the other of us will
yet pull you away from the ranch.
Which pole of the magnet will be the
stronger, I wonder.

Your loving

EUNICE

P. S.—You would never guess whom
I saw this morning. I was hurrying
up to the Conservatory. The elevator
was crowded, and, just as some one
pushed me rudely—I'm not fast
enough for New York yet—I found an
arm put out to protect me, and in a
moment the crowd had pressed me so
close to Leroy Ellerton I could hardly
see his face. He put his arm between
me and the crowd to shield me. I was
so glad to see him, for I am a bit lonely

here, when I look for a familiar face in
the crowd.

I thought he went abroad in October,
but it seems he didn't go.   He said he
had to stay here and look after his
father's business, said he had to give up
all that beautiful trip to Italy he had
told you and me about before he left
Talton in September.   How long ago
it seems now since I was at home and
Leroy was our guest.   He is coming
Sunday to take me to hear a great
soloist at one of the big churches.   One
has such opportunities for those things
here.   Oh, I am sure I shall like it more
and more.   But when it comes to saying good-bye, dear Papa, I am not real
sure about that past incarnation.   But
let it stand.   I remember what you said
when I left home: "If I would study
hard and if I liked it here, I might stay
as long as I pleased."   I 'll tell you
later about that.

                          EUNICE

Letter from LEROY ELLERTON, New York, to JOHN ELLER- TON, Liverpool.

NEW YORK, *November.*

DEAR FATHER:

I am doing very well with the office work, although I'll be mighty glad when your ship steams in again. I read all you wrote about what I was missing by not trotting after you to Europe in October, as I promised to do when I left Kansas. Great guns! Dad, it was your own fault I did not go at once. Your cablegram keeping me here for a month was waiting for me when I got in from the West. I confess it didn't look bad to me, though, to read that I would be needed in the office here for a short time. I stayed willingly, because the old Atlantic had a sort of impass- able look every time I saw it. And now you try to make me feel what I'm losing by not accepting this offer from you to tour Italy in December and January. I reckon Italy will be stick- ing on the map yet a while, and I can see it 'most any old December or Janu- ary, unless Vesuvius takes a notion to blow it up. In that case I'm safer here anyhow.

By the way, old Bronson's daughter, the "green Kansas girl," you called her, is in New York now studying voice culture. Don't turn up your aristocratic nose and ask how a Kaw squaw can do anything with voice culture. It makes me wrathy with my paternal relative every time I think of how you regard Eunice Bronson. I met her in an up-town elevator this morning. I mean she met me, for I saw her come from her train and meet our friends, and I saw where they lodged her. In fact, I've been pretty much awake to every move she has made in New York. But to-day we came together in an elevator where a metropolitan hog was about to jostle the timid little Western girl off the edge of the earth.

She thought I had gone abroad, but I told her I was looking after your business. That's straight goods, Daddy; I'm managing your estate and I wasn't telling any story. You'll say I could drop it any half-minute and join you if I chose. But I don't choose — not right now anyhow.

Yours aff.,

LEROY

DECEMBER

Letter from EUNICE BRONSON, New York, to DANIEL BRON-SON, Kansas.

NEW YORK, *Christmas Eve.*

DEAR FATHER:

It is Christmas Eve, — such a cold white Yule-time as I can hardly remember in Kansas. And I remember everything that ever happened in my life in the West, although I am thoroughly acclimated here, and feel as if I might have lived here forever.

Yet always I'm thinking of you and Seth. And especially to-night, my first holiday season away from home. I do so much wish you a happy Christmas, Father. There's a misgiving down in my heart as I write this. Can you have a real happy Christmas with both of us away? Is your heart in the ranch house on the Solomon to-night? Or is it half in Seattle with my big brother, and half in New York with me?

I don't blame Seth for going West. That is a man's right. But I am not sure of myself to-night. Ought I to be at home with my lonely father? It puts a sadness in this Christmas Eve for me. And yet, I remember how you delighted in all my plans for coming East, and every letter you write is so full of inter-

est in my work, and hope that I may
win. I guess you love your little girl
too much for either of us to be unhappy.
And I am going to win, Father. That's
what I came here to do. I am studying
hard. I never worked in that farm
house in the days when the crops failed
and we couldn't afford to hire help as
I am working now. But I am so happy
in it all, it hardly seems like work. And
as to liking New York — I love it. I
have found so many pleasant people.
New friends do not crowd out old ones
at all. I find room for both. Leroy
has been very kind to me and I've had
such a round of good things I've been
in a perfect whirl. I can't realize
sometimes that I am the same Kansas
girl who came to New York last Fall.
Life here is so different, so hurried and
feverish, I wonder where it will lead to,
sometimes. Yet, I like it for this very
hurry.

And here is your letter saying you'll
send me to Europe where I may study
all next year if I like. Of course, I
want to go to Europe. It is the dream
of all my years. Everybody says my
success is assured if only I can get a
little foreign training. You would be
so proud of me if I made a name for
myself as a singer. And I shall try so
hard to earn a great name.

Leroy was here last night. He is a
full-fledged business man now. We

talked of the trip to Europe. Somehow he is more enthusiastic than anybody else about my going, but he never mentions the matter unless I bring it up, and he always changes the subject. But when he does talk he just makes Europe out a perfect paradise of opportunity and urges me to go, even when I tell him how lonely you will be without me.

My teachers here say that I must have had very fine instruction before coming to them, or I could not have made such progress in so short a time here, nor give such promise of results when I go abroad. Of course, I know I had good teachers.

What do you suppose Leroy said to me to-night? He came over to wish me the season's greeting, and to bring me a big bunch of the most exquisite roses I ever saw. When I told him what the professor at the Conservatory had said of my training, he replied:

"It's because you sang so much in the open air. It was the prairie that put tone and volume into your voice."

I answered that it was my good college training.

"It takes the West to put foundation under the East," I said jokingly.

"Yes, and it takes some Western folks to knock the foundation out from under some of us," Leroy answered, and changed the subject.

It is getting late and the Christmas bells will be chiming soon their old, old music of "peace on earth,—good will to men." Peace and good will, and all a daughter's love, I am sending to you so far away in the Solomon Valley to-night, where the world is still and full of peace. The roar in New York seems never to stop. I am going to get away out of it for a little moment and dream myself back in the home with you.

Father, may I tell you a secret? I have nobody but you to whom I can write or speak. I wish I didn't care so much for what Leroy thinks. But I do. He does not know—will never know. He is wrapped up in this busy life of the city. And he is making money. He doesn't care whether I go to Berlin or Talton. It all began last Summer. I tried to think I should forget it when he was gone. I put all my heart into my work and I'm keeping it there, for that is my life. So, giving it up now would be like giving up my life. And yet, sometimes, I've dreamed of how a home might be with one I most loved there.

But there is no use to think of what might be. What is, is a hard-hearted, cool-spirited, city-bred business man, engrossed heart and soul in dollars and cents and the great rushing crowd of a tremendous city, of which he is a part; and a maiden—destined to be a maiden always — who longs for the success that must come, a name of world-wide note, and the fame that is honestly won and belongs to those who do great things.

Father dear, you must never tell that I told you this about Roy. It is a relief to tell you. Now it is written, I feel better.

When I get all my plans for Europe arranged, I 'll write them in full. Are you sure you won't miss me too much?

These beautiful roses fill the air with their perfume. They are dainty and pink like the pink tints of a twilight sky that I 've seen above the prairies beyond Waconda. * * *

Midnight, and the Christmas bells are chiming now. They seem to voice my love to you, dear, far-away Father, so good to me. I hope these sweet-toned bells bring dreams of peace to all I love — you and Seth — and even to Leroy, who is not thinking of me as they chime. He is dreaming of the business success he is to achieve. Peace and good will, and all good things be yours.

Lovingly,

EUNICE

Letter from **LEROY ELLERTON**
to his **MOTHER**

NEW YORK, *Christmas Eve.*
DEAR, DEAR MOTHER:

My Christmas greeting to you this
white, clear Christmas eve, not by letter nor cable, but by that wireless line
of love vibrating from the heart of every
boy who loves his mother as I do you.
And equal greeting and love to my
father with you — but it's a different
kind of affection.   You know a fellow's
mother is his *mother,* that's all.   And
if it wasn't Christmastide and I had the
chance, I'd like to punch the old gentleman a round or two just to paste time
out of him, as the boys say, for the low-
down trick he played on me last Spring.

To think of him and Daniel Bronson
being boy playmates and old college
chums at Yale, the lobsters!   And of
sending me, all verdant and innocent,
out to Kansas to make a fool of myself.
Well, it was a good thing the Atlantic
was between us when I read your letter,
explaining everything.   As I say, it's
the Yule time of love, so I'll be mild.
Only, if old Vesuvius should get to acting ugly, keep him on the landward side
of you.   He ought to be shaken up and
likewise scorched and have sackcloth
and ashes for his portion for a while.

I've tried to think of all the silly, snobbish things I said at the Bronsons' last April and May — tried to forget them rather, for they come back to my mind often enough. I'm glad I had the sense to get over it all before many weeks and to see how the land lay. I inherited that sense from you, dearie (Dad hasn't that much altogether, let alone giving me any), and I quit acting the idiot pretty early in the game. But it is the hour of peace on earth and good will to men. I wish the angels had made it women too, and not in irreverence, I wish it.

Mother dear, I must tell you some things to-night, just as I used to tell you my troubles when I was a little boy and cuddled down by your knee on winter evenings. Let me feel your hand on my hair again as I write.

I learned more than father had thought about in Kansas last Summer. He wanted me to find out what the West is like. That rheumatism business was only a side issue with him. It did get me away from thinking of my own ailments. I'm doubly grateful for that. Heaven save us from a whining man! — or anybody else who dotes on "symptoms" and keeps his pains posted up for public inspection. Ellerton, Senior, wanted me to find out the worth of character in rural homes and

country lives. I found it out. Give
me 99 per cent plus on Exhibit " A."

Mother, I found more than that. I
saw clearly the way of life I want to go.
It is in my New England blood to love
the soil. Am I not the son of Vermont
and Maine, both of my parents born
and reared away from the city? I
wakened to my kingdom one day out
on the Kansas prairies. It began by
finding fault with Seth Bronson for not
wanting to stay on the ranch with his
father. What he was turning down
seemed so full of promise to me. I
love those grand, open fields on the
sunny plains. The growing crops and
fattening stock, the bounty of Nature,
and the chance to *think* and *live* all
called to me as nothing else in this world
ever did — or ever will.

Yes, I'm fixed here, in the city, with
one foot lariated to an office desk-leg,
and I shall pay out my rope as far as
the parks, now and then in the spring
and summer time, while out in Kansas,
the

"Rolling prairie's billowy swell,
Breezy upland, and timbered dell,
Stately mansion, and hut forlorn —
All are hidden by walls of corn."

I'm trying heart and soul to be the
junior partner here and to do my work

well. And I'll keep on till it is second nature to me.

There was another lesson I learned in the West, one that Father didn't know was in the book, or he might not have selected the Solomon Valley as a sanitarium for me. Let me whisper, Mummy. I learned to love a dear, sweet-faced country girl, a wide-awake, capable, fun-loving, but scholarly, thinking girl. A girl with a life purpose of her own — ding it! — a plan for the future so big and definite that I cut no figure in it. I've told you about Eunice Bronson and her notion of being a musician. She is here now, taking voice culture under New York's Best. Said Best are wild about her, urging her to keep to this purpose she brought with her. Study here and abroad! Training under the best Masters of Europe! I hear it all the time.

For I stay pretty close to her here. You can guess why I turned down Italy this year. I'm a fool still. Father'll have to play a bigger trick yet to get me altogether cured. I'm going to stay here too, as long as she is in New York. It is my last, last time, you see. Also, you can see how there is nothing for me in the Solomon Valley now, even if I could cut this business career.

Have I told her all this? Not I. I tried to when we were at Waconda

Springs one August evening. But I
read her story first and I knew it would
be wasted time, so I kept still. I had
hope then, of something changing
things. I haven't any more. She is
planning to go to Europe in June.
When her steamer sails, it will carry
my one dream of happiness with it. So,
I'm going to keep her near me as long
as I can; and when she gets ready to
leave New York, I'll slip up to Montreal for a fortnight, so I can't play the
—— blamed fool and go with her.
It would be like me. I'm such a ——
chump. And then when she is out in
mid-ocean, I'll come back and resume
my fetters here.

But, mother darling, I'll play the
man and make my bondage my help.
I'm not going to be a silly kind of idiot.
I'll just do the best work possible and
you and father will be proud of me as
a business man some day, I hope.

.   .   .   .

The Christmas bells are chiming, so
it is midnight. This is the strangest
Christmas I have ever known. The only
peace on earth for me, dear mother, is
the peace of overcoming. Surely there
will be a day when I'll forget all this
and be as happy as I used to be.
Life has these rifts, I know. But the
chasms close again, don't they? * * *
There are the bells again, so sweet and

clear. I hope they are sounding softly in dreams for Eunice, who is dreaming of fame, not of me. To you and father, far away, a joyous Christmas. And to all the world, from Leroy Ellerton, good will and peace.

Good-night and good-morning, precious Mother.

Lovingly,

Roy

Letter from DANIEL BRONSON,
Kansas, to EUNICE BRON-
SON, New York

KANSAS, *Christmas Eve.*
DEAR DAUGHTER EUNICE:

This is Christmas Eve, and although I am all alone, I am happy to send Christmas greeting to my children. I sent all the Christmas gifts by express a week ago, so you will be sure to have them in the morning. The house seems pretty big and hollow-sounding, for it is the first time in a quarter of a century that I have been alone when the holiday season came.

It seems such a little while ago that you and Seth were toddling about in our little two-roomed house. That's the tool-house now. Ellerton, your oldest brother, was born in a dugout one Christmas Eve, twenty-four years ago. Poor, little baby! He didn't live the summer through. We had a better home — a palace it was to your mother and me — when you and Seth came to us. And yet, how poor we were! No Christmas stockings in those first years. We just kept Christmas in our hearts, which isn't a bad place, Eunice, to celebrate it. For we were happy in each other's love, my wife and I, and in our two sturdy little ones, who never knew what sickness meant. These things made up for the lack of beautiful gifts. Such a little while ago all that was. And now Christmas Eve is here again. The quarter section of land I preëmpted on the frontier is only one-eighth of the Bronson ranch to-day. The little dugout is the dog-house now, and the 12 x 14 homestead, a vine-covered tool shelter. Fourteen rooms, and upper and lower verandas, hot and cold water, a lighting and heating system, etc., etc. These things have grown up from year to year.

But to-night, although I am utterly alone, daughter dear, I won't say I am lonely, for I know my children's hearts are with me. And space does n't count where love is strong.

Seth writes that it is bitterly cold in Seattle, and I see by the daily papers that New York will have a white Christmas. Out here the air is almost balmy, and the skies are cloudless. There is a sort of October haze over the landscape, a sweet restfulness and peace that seem to pervade everything.

I had business over Waconda way to-day. It was sunset when I reached the Springs coming home. I was in no hurry, for there were no little children waiting at home for me to-night.

So, I turned aside and went over to Waconda while the sun sank from sight and the twilight of this beautiful Christmas Eve came on. My heart that had been sore and aching for my children was at peace as I sat on the rocks and thought of you.

Seth is more than making good, he writes, and is infatuated with Seattle. It seems a certain black-eyed Manhattan girl, a classmate of his, has gone to Seattle in the interests of Domestic Science, and Seth, also in the interests of Domestic Science, is finding that city a good location. As I sat by the "Spirit Springs," as we used to call it, and watched the changing beauty of the twilight, I lived my youth over again until my own heart-ache slipped away. For love is a divine thing.

"The love of home and native land,
And that which springs 'twixt son
and sire,
And that which welds the heart and
hand
Of man and maiden in its fire
Are signs by which we understand
The Love whose passion shook the
Cross;
And all those loves that deep and broad
Make princely gain or priceless loss,
Reveal the Love that lives in God
As in a blood-illumined gloss."

I thought of my daughter away to the eastward. I know, Eunice, that your heart is full of joy to-night, because New York holds the best things in the world for you now, although you have put away the things that are making my boy's Christmas good. You will come back to them some day, when fame and success are won. God grant you do not return too late. There comes a time to all of us when the sweetest peace we can know is the peace of overcoming; of forgetting ourselves in our love for our fellow man.

Believe me, dearie, there wasn't a happier man in all Kansas to-night than your old farmer father, driving home in the quiet evening time. I lifted my face to the open skies and looked into the faces of the stars, the same old stars that watched this valley long before Waconda was here, and down through countless centuries while bald rock became sandy desert, and sandy desert grew to grassy plain, and grassy plain to verdant prairie, which human hands—even my hands—have helped to turn to fruitful fields, for a happy folk to thrive upon.

And back of these changeless stars is the changeless love of the Heavenly Father. His right hand has guided me down the years. I love the land where I have walked with Him in storm and sunshine; so the Christmas peace and good will are blessing the Solomon Valley for me.

.　.　.　.　.　.　.　.　.

It is growing late — almost midnight. May the love of God, the Father Almighty, and of Jesus Christ, His Son, be and abide with my children now and through the coming years.

Your affectionate father,

DANIEL BRONSON

JUNE

*Letter from EUNICE BRONSON,
Talton, Kansas, to LEROY EL-
LERTON, New York City.*

TALTON, KANSAS, *June.*

MY DEAR FRIEND:

Here I am again out on the ranch in
the Solomon Valley. Of course you,
with all of my New York friends, will
be utterly disappointed in me, for my
career was so full of promise. And
father had given full consent for me to
go on with my music under German
masters. Oh, it was a rosy world open-
ing before me, full of busy days, of
struggling onward, winning my way
step by step, and maybe too, full of
rivalry and much defeat before fame
came. For that was what I wanted—
or thought I wanted—the sound of
praise, the cheering audiences, the
power of mastery over listening minds,
the rush and whirl and glitter of a grand
career.

When you went up to Montreal on
business just before I was ready to sail,
I don't know what led me to stop long
enough to sit down and take stock of
myself. But I did. I weighed Life
as if it were calculated in ounces and
pounds. And the result was this: I
gave up every plan and hope and

dream and came back again to Kansas, because my father wanted me and needed me. He didn't tell me so. Brave old farmer that he is! He learned long ago how to endure and not complain. One gleans that lesson from the prairie sod in the years when the sunshine is a furnace and the clouds forget their rain and the fierce winds blow all the seed away from the loose, dusty earth. In such years the farmers wait unchanged like Waconda, sure that other seasons will bring fruition of their hopes. And so my father waited, filling every letter with cheery words. He sent me all the funds I needed and put no bar in the way of my doing just as I chose.

Give me credit, or blame me alone, for turning my face from the East. And don't be too severe, please, for I have valued your friendship. And now that you are a fixture in the city, a wheel in the great machinery of its business, and I am only a home-maker in a Kansas farm house, our lives will run so far apart, it will be by merest chance of Fate that they will ever cross lines again. Please do not think I am making an utter failure of living. Remember me kindly if you remember at all. I told you once out by Waconda, the message of whose waters I could never understand, that we must read life, each for himself. I do not know why that piece of the green ocean is held here in the heart of the green prairie, but I do know that my work is here with my father and home and the best folks on earth — these lifetime neighbors and friends — who are a part of this Solomon River country.

If you could only see how this home looks to my eyes that I thought could never grow weary of city grandeur, and if you could see the vast, beautiful outdoor world unrolling its June splendor, you would be gentle in your thought of me. The call of the West was in my ears day and night, much as I tried to drown it with the noise of the city and the roar of the Atlantic and the cries of Fame urging me on. The bustle of New York, the fever for a career, go down, for me before the duties of home; and the handsome parks, the huge buildings, the rushing crowds, all give place to the wide Kansas prairies and the peace of the Solomon Valley. You will be disappointed in me, and disgusted with me. But while I miss many things I have been having for nearly a year, I am finding real life here, and rest, and — well, you know, I was born in Kansas, and after all, I'm happiest here.

Yours sincerely,

EUNICE BRONSON

P. S.—Strangely enough, I can reach
the high notes here when I sing out on
the open prairie that I never could
reach in the Conservatory. My voice
is richest here. So, I must belong in
the heart of Kansas.

EUNICE

Letter from LEROY ELLERTON, Talton, Kansas, to JOHN EL- LERTON, Liverpool

TALTON, KANSAS, *June.*

MY DEAR FATHER:

Don't be surprised when you get this, not too surprised, anyhow. I send this to Liverpool so you may know what to expect when you get to New York. I'm out hunting the rheumatism I lost here once.

You see, Father, I came West first against my will, for I am a born New Yorker, that is to say I was a narrow provincial. It didn't take many weeks for me to learn my lesson — that this is the real thing, not mere sham living, as I had supposed it would be. More than that, I found the dearest girl in the world out here. I lost my rheuma- tism and heart at the same time. And I learned to detest the city jungle as I learned to love this valley. The only thing I have ever really wanted to do is to put my whole energy into the life and work of a Kansas ranch. Maybe nobody ever heard of a city boy want- ing to become a farmer. Let me tell you that lazy Leroy Ellerton never really lived in any city; he just stayed there to be with his parents and give dignity to the family through his infancy and boyhood, and until he had finished college. One day, out in

the Solomon Valley, his real self awoke,
and clamored for its rights. Day by
day through a glorious Summer he saw
more and more clearly the work his
heart and hand were yearning for.
There are so many misfits in this world,
the wonder is there is any success at all.
So many "square men in round holes,"
etc., and the trouble generally comes in
trying to make a "rounder" of the
square man instead of working a little
on the hole he must fit into.

Anyhow, the same Leroy boy knew
eternally well what he could do best and
was just planning to negotiate matters
for getting into it, when there came the
decree that he must give it up. And
he gave it up, knowing, like Kipling's
fool, when he did it that—

"*Part of him lived, but most of him
died.*"

But I obeyed to a degree. I tried
honestly to do your bidding. When I
had left Kansas and reached the city,
intending to take the steamer the next
day for Liverpool, your cablegram kept
me back for a brief time. Then Eunice
came to New York, and somehow a
pleasure trip through Italy looked like
hard work at once, and I cut it out. But
I buckled down to real hard labor,
and I worked all the harder to fill my
place with you when Eunice thought
her pleasure lay in a singer's career. I
never tried to persuade her away from

it. She gave it up herself, and came back to make her home in Kansas and to make her father happy. And the joy of duty done was hers.

When Eunice was ready to sail for Europe, I knew I'd make a fool of myself if I stayed visibly in New York. So, I told her I was going to Montreal on business. I knew in a thousand years the Ellertons had never had any business in Montreal. But I told her that, intending to hide around a corner.

That wasn't going to work, I soon found out, so I put off — on a penance pilgrimage to East Machias, Maine.

Father, I understand now all about the reward of humble sacrifice. I went up to cheer Aunt Prudence in her lonely hours. And it happened that Aunt Pru was the one to confer benefits. One evening, sitting in the twilight by the wood fire, somehow — Lord knows — the dear old lady drew me on and on to talk to her as I never dreamed of talking to anybody but my own Mummy.

And then, with the firelight on her sweet old face and her snowy hair and with the wisdom of her eighty years of thoughtful living and good deeds to others, she seemed a sort of saint to me.

"Eunice isn't doing her duty to her father, so much as to herself," Aunt Pru declared. "Far down in the girl's heart there is a voice calling her away

from all this thing she has planned, or
she could not leave it. Take my word,
Leroy, the girl isn't happy here, and
she knows where her duty lies."

"But what should I do, Aunt Prudence?" I asked her.

"The work you can do best and love
the doing. It's not always the easiest
work, as labor goes, nor the work that
brings the most money, but if it's the
thing you love to do, and can work the
prettiest pattern into it, do that."

Then I saw my duty. Father, I
hate Wall Street, and I've come out
here to live a broad, busy, free life, to be
a farmer in the Solomon Valley. To
the life I leave behind me in the city, it
is as health to fever; as peace after tur-
moil. This is the best place on earth
for me, for while our families are widely
separated—you and mother in New
York and Seth Bronson in Seattle—
they centre here.

I know all about your friendship for
Daniel Bronson, you two old sinners!
I ought to be obliged to you for letting
me make a fool of myself, for it was
good for me, maybe. Only nobody,
least of all a New Yorker, cares to
make a fool of himself. I came here
two days ago. Last night we went in
the auto over to that same lost bit of
the sea, I wrote you about last year—I
mean Waconda Springs.

Sitting on the rocks looking out

toward the Solomon River, we saw the full moon make a new heaven and a new earth for this exquisite June night. I asked Eunice again, as I had asked her once before, if she knew the mystery of old Waconda, and the message of the waters to us.

"I cannot understand why this spring was left here all these years," she said. "It is a mystery I could never fathom."

And then I told her what the waters had told me; that this tiny bit of the sea, left here for so many centuries, had so loved this place, so rested in the peace and beauty of the valley, sun-kissed and mist-swathed, with the tenderness of the springtime, the glory of mid-summer, the splendor of autumn, that it chose to stay here; chose to forsake the restless, stormy, seething ocean that hammers forever on its shores and here to watch the unfolding of a kingdom, the life of a people coming at last into their own.

The clear green water dimpled in silver sparkles under the glorious moon, and the peace of the Solomon Valley mingled with the peace of our own hearts. For we, too, had found our own at last, — our kingdom here in Kansas.

Your loving

ROY

CPSIA information can be obtained
at www.ICGtesting.com
Printed in the USA
LVOW13*0234030818
585826LV00015B/192/P